Around Town:
Things You Can Do in Your Community

Four Procedural Texts

by Katherine Scraper with Jeremiah White, Jayne Cavender, Trinity Daniels, and Destiny Johnson

Table of Contents

Focus on the Genre: Procedural Text 2

Meet the Student-Authors 4

Your Community in Pictures 6

Time for a Haircut! 8

Have Fun! Make Money!
How to Set Up a Popcorn Stand 10

How to Buy a Pet Fish 12

The Writer's Craft: Procedural Text 14

Glossary 16

Make Connections Across Texts . . . . Inside Back Cover

FOCUS ON THE GENRE

Procedural Text

What is a procedural text?

A procedural text is writing that tells how to make or do something. We use procedural texts every day! We make soup using a recipe in a cookbook. We learn new math skills by following the steps in a textbook. We learn to play new board games by reading the rules that come in the box. Adults use procedural texts at home, in their jobs, and in their hobbies. Other names for procedural texts are technical writing, instructions, directions, or how-to's.

What is the purpose of a procedural text?

A procedural text describes how to do something the author is good at in a way that other people can understand. The author clearly explains what supplies and equipment to use and what steps to follow. Some authors share tips they've learned from personal experience that will help the process go more smoothly for readers. The author usually includes one or more photographs, illustrations, or diagrams to help readers visualize, or see, how to do the steps. Sometimes the author includes a picture of the finished product as well.

Who is the audience for a procedural text?

Procedural texts are for everyone! People of all ages use procedural texts to learn new skills, perform science experiments, administer first aid, build, cook or bake foods, play games, create crafts, or improve their abilities in music or sports. People can find procedural texts in books, magazines, newspapers, pamphlets, instructions that come with purchases, and on the Internet.

Features of a Procedural Text

- The title clearly identifies the topic.
- The author includes photographs, illustrations, or diagrams to help explain the process.
- The introduction tells why the reader will want to make or do the activity or project.
- Most sentences begin with verbs. The sentences are short and direct.
- Supplies and equipment are listed in the order in which they are used.
- The directions are given as numbered steps or short paragraphs with sequence words.

How do you read a procedural text?

You can choose a procedural text by its title. The title will tell you what you can learn to make or do by reading the text. Next, check the list of supplies and equipment to see if you have everything you need. After that, read through all the steps and study the pictures to make sure you understand what to do. Then—begin! As you work, pay special attention to any tips the author provides.

Meet the Student-Authors

"Your Community in Pictures"
by Jeremiah White

"It's fun to explore your community with a digital camera. If a shot doesn't turn out, you can easily delete it . . . On the other hand, you might end up with a masterpiece!"

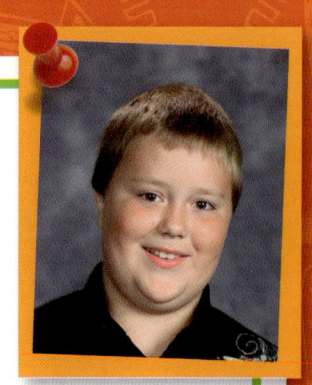

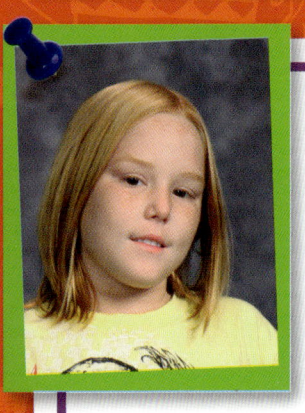

"Time for a Haircut!"
by Jayne Cavender

"I make my own haircut appointments, but my mom goes with me. I like getting to know the barber and other community workers while we're out running errands."

"How to Buy a Pet Fish"
by Destiny Johnson

"Fish are good pets for any size home. You can buy fish at pet stores and department stores in most communities."

"Have Fun! Make Money! How to Set Up a Popcorn Stand"

by Trinity Daniels

"Microwave popcorn is easy to make and easy to sell. I work at a Survivor Sale in the fall—a huge yard sale where we raise money to help cancer patients pay for transportation to their treatment facilities. Last year we had a hot dog stand. Next time we plan to sell popcorn instead."

Jeremiah, Jayne, Destiny, and Trinity attend Lincoln Elementary School in El Dorado, Kansas.

Tools Writers Use

A Strong Lead

The opening section, or introduction, of a text is called the lead. The lead tells you something about the subject and hints at what you may learn. A strong lead grabs or "hooks" readers and makes them want to keep reading. Writers use two types of leads. A direct lead tells what the piece is about and why the topic is important. An indirect lead may quote someone, ask a question, describe something, or tell an anecdote, or true story, about the topic.

Your Community in Pictures

Your school . . . the park . . . the ball field . . . the zoo . . . stores . . . historic buildings . . . all these and more provide opportunities to take digital photos in your community. I'll tell you how to use your camera and save your pictures on a computer, but the rest is up to you. Ready? Here we go!

1. Get a camera that's easy to carry so you can take it with you wherever you go. The **least complicated** time to take photos is when you're walking somewhere, but sometimes you can get some good shots from a car or bus window.

✽ **TIPS: Make sure the camera is charged, and carry a set of fresh batteries.**

2. Choose something you want to take a picture of. Find a subject (a person, place, or object) that you really like.

▲ I call this the goose park because of all the ducks and geese.

▲ This is my school.

3. Turn your camera on. Center the view window on the subject. Zoom in or out if needed, and then push the button on top of the camera.

✱ **TIP: Try to take several shots of the same thing in case some of the pictures don't turn out.**

4. Once you get back home, get out the transfer cord. Put the small end in the camera and the larger end in your computer. Follow the prompts on your camera and computer screens to transfer the photos.

5. Sort through the photos and delete any you don't want to keep. Label the rest and put them in a folder on your computer.

6. Look for opportunities to share your most appealing, **most unique**, or **wackiest** photos. However, be sure to ask an adult in your family before printing the photos or posting them online.

▲ The county rebuilt the clock on the courthouse tower when I was around eight years old.

▲ Freddy's is my favorite place to eat.

▲ Here's my favorite place to go—the movie theater.

Time for a Haircut!

Do you know any of your town's barbers or hairstylists? I do! It's fun to chat with them while they're cutting my hair. Haircutters are often among the **most sociable** people around! They seem to have their finger on the pulse of the community. Anyway, here is how to get a haircut in your community:

1. Call your favorite hair salon or barbershop for an appointment. Ask an adult to take you to the shop. Give the person at the counter your name. While you're waiting, you can look at magazines—including some that have cool hairstyles.

* **TIP: If you go to a walk-in shop, try to arrive when it will be the least occupied. For example, opening time Saturday morning is usually better than afternoon.**

2. When it's your turn, the barber/hairstylist will call your name and show you where to sit. While he puts a smock over you, he'll ask what type of haircut you want. Describe the style the best you can, or bring a picture to show him.

3. Sit still as the barber cuts your hair, but feel free to chat. When the barber is done, check the front, sides, and back of your hair in the mirror. Then you're ready to go.

4. Pay the barber. If you can, leave a tip. (Usually, around 10–20 percent of the price is the proper thing to do—unless the barber is the owner, in which case you don't need to leave a tip.) Be sure to say "thank you"! Now . . . go show off your new haircut!

▲ my new hairdo

Reread the Procedural Texts

Analyze the Texts
- What is the purpose of these two procedural texts? How does each text relate to the title of the book?
- Neither author lists supplies and equipment at the beginning of their texts. Why?
- Both authors use numbered steps. How do these make the procedural texts easier to read?
- What sequence words and phrases do the authors use? How do these help readers better understand the processes?
- How do the authors use art to support their texts? What did you learn from the captions?

Analyze the Tools Writers Use: A Strong Lead
- What type of lead does each author use? How do you know?
- Do the authors' leads "hook" you as a reader? Why or why not?
- What did you expect to learn after reading each lead?
- How else could the first author have started the text? The second author?

Focus on Words: Superlatives

Superlatives are special adjectives that are used to compare three or more things. Some superlatives end in **–est**, while others are preceded by the word **most** or **least**. Make a chart like the one below. Analyze the superlatives in the first two procedural texts. Then record what each superlative describes. For example, the superlative **most appealing** (page 7) describes the noun **photos**.

Page	Superlative	What It Describes
6	least complicated	
7	most unique	
7	wackiest	
8	most sociable	
8	least occupied	

Have Fun! Make Money!
How to Set Up a Popcorn Stand

The author clearly states her topic in the title. She gives it a catchy title to get readers' attention.

Do you want to make money for a worthy cause in your community? A popcorn stand is the perfect way to go!

Things You Will Need
- poster board
- markers
- several bags of microwave popcorn
- microwave
- folding table
- tape

The bulleted list shows readers what supplies they will need and in what order they will use them.

What to Do

Decide when and where you'll have your popcorn stand. (Get permission from the sponsoring organization or place to sell.) Ask your friends and family—including at least one adult—to help out. Use the poster board and markers to make signs advertising your popcorn stand.

1.
2.
3.

On the day of the event, make the popcorn. Here's how:

1. Remove the plastic wrap from the popcorn bag, but don't open it. Unfold the packet and put it in the microwave.

2. Set the microwave for four minutes (or whatever the directions on the bag say) and push START.

3. Don't go away! Instead, listen to the popcorn pop. Remember that popping times are estimates. If several seconds of silence pass between pops, stop the microwave, or else the popcorn might burn.

4. Grab the popcorn bag from the microwave, but be careful—it will be HOT! Open the bag away from your face and pour the popcorn into a large bowl. Keep popping popcorn until you have all you need.

5. Make individual bags or boxes of popcorn. Once your popcorn is ready to be sold, deliver it to your stand (folding table), hang the signs with the tape, and you're in business. Have fun, and good luck!

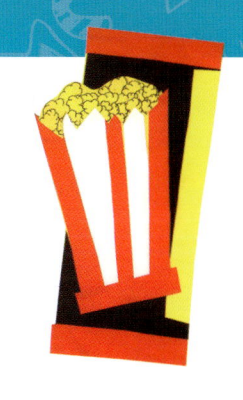

The author includes tips to motivate readers and help them be more successful with their project.

✽ TIPS: *A good place to have a popcorn stand is at a yard sale. Besides a well-chosen location, the* **most profitable** *popcorn stands feature the* **freshest** *popcorn,* **most attractive** *signs, and* **friendliest** *kids.*

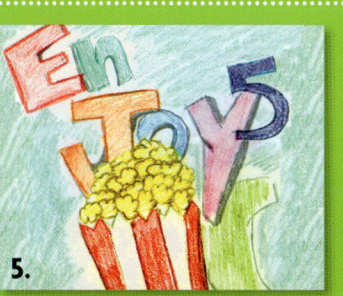

4.

5.

A series of illustrations helps readers visualize important steps in the process.

How to Buy a Pet Fish

The author gives a brief introduction to interest readers in the topic.

The author uses numbered steps to clearly show readers what to do.

The author uses active verbs to keep the instructions short and direct.

A fish is one of the **most pleasant** pets you can own. Find a pet store in your community, and follow these steps to get started:

1. Before you go to the store, think about the space you have for a fish and the amount of time you want to put into caring for it.
2. When you are at the store, ask a worker to help you choose the **most suitable** fish. Then you will need to purchase a bowl or tank for the fish to live in. Get some rocks for the bottom of the tank, and ask for tips on cleaning it.
3. The worker will put the fish in a bag of water. Find out how long you can leave the fish in the bag before you must put it in the tank. Then ask what type of fish food to buy and how much and how often to feed your fish.
4. Take the fish home. Put water in the tank and put the rocks in the bottom. Release the fish into the tank. Add fish food. Enjoy watching your new finny friend explore its new home. Continue feeding your fish at the right time, and make sure the tank is always at its **tidiest**. Your fish will thank you!

✸ **TIP: Even if you live in a "No Pets" apartment, you can usually get permission for a fish.**

Reread the Procedural Texts

Analyze the Texts
- Look at the titles for these procedural texts. How do they differ?
- The author of the popcorn stand text includes a list of supplies and equipment. How did she decide what to list first? Last?
- Both authors use numbered steps. Could any steps be completed in a different order? Explain.
- The author uses the word **continue** in the fish text. What does that word suggest?
- How did the authors use graphic and text features to support their texts? What did you learn from the tips?

Analyze the Tools Writers Use: A Strong Lead
- What type of lead does each author use? How do you know?
- What part of the leads "hooked" you? Explain.
- What did you expect to learn after reading each lead?
- What are some other ways to start a procedural text?

Focus on Words: Superlatives
Make a chart like the one below. Analyze the superlatives in the last two procedural texts. Then record what each superlative describes. For example, the superlative **friendliest** (page 11) describes the noun **kids**.

Page	Superlative	What It Describes
11	most profitable	
11	freshest	
11	most attractive	
12	most pleasant	
12	most suitable	
12	tidiest	

The Writer's Craft

How does an author write a
Procedural Text?

Reread "Have Fun! Make Money! How to Set Up a Popcorn Stand" and think about what Trinity Daniels did to write this procedural text. How did she explain the activity in a way readers could understand? How can you, as a writer, develop your own procedural text?

1. Decide on an Activity or Project

Remember, a procedural text describes something the author knows how to do well. In this text, the author wants to tell readers how to raise money by selling popcorn. She includes a brief introduction explaining why readers may want to do this activity.

2. Decide What Supplies and Equipment to Use

If your activity needs supplies or equipment, create a bulleted list. List each item in the order readers will use it.

3. Decide What Steps to Use

You can write using numbered steps or short paragraphs with sequencing words. Begin sentences with verbs, and use short, direct sentences. Ask yourself:

- Which method—numbered steps or short paragraphs—will be clearer to my audience?
- If I use numbered steps, how will I order them?
- If I use paragraphs, how will I divide them? What sequencing words will I use to make my steps logical?
- Do I need to include any tips to help readers be successful? If so, where should I put them?

4. Decide What Art to Use

Pictures help readers visualize how to do the activity and show what the finished product looks like. Ask yourself:

- What photographs could I take as I go through the steps? What photographs could someone take of me working?
- What illustrations would help readers understand the steps?
- What diagrams could I use to explain one or more steps?
- What art could I add as I go? What art could I put at the end?
- What captions or labels could I add to my art?

5. Field-Test Your Writing

Ask a friend to read and try your activity. Write down anything that confuses your friend or any questions he or she asks. Use this information to add needed supplies, equipment, steps, tips, or art to your procedural writing.

Activity or Project	raising money by selling popcorn
Things I Need	poster board, markers, microwave popcorn, microwave, folding table, tape
Steps	choose a location; make signs; make popcorn; set up; sell popcorn
Art	illustrations of steps

Glossary

freshest — (FREH-shest) made most recently; newest (page 11)

least complicated — (LEEST KAHM-plih-kay-ted) easiest; simplest to do (page 6)

least occupied — (LEEST AH-kyuh-pide) having the fewest people (page 8)

most attractive — (MOST uh-TRAK-tiv) most beautiful and appealing (page 11)

most pleasant — (MOST PLEH-zent) most enjoyable and satisfying (page 12)

most profitable — (MOST PRAH-fih-tuh-bul) making the most money (page 11)

most sociable — (MOST SOH-shuh-bul) friendliest; best at being around other people (page 8)

most suitable — (MOST SOO-tuh-bul) best, or just right, for you (page 12)

most unique — (MOST yoo-NEEK) most special in a singular way (page 7)

tidiest — (TY-dee-est) neatest and cleanest (page 12)

wackiest — (WA-kee-est) silliest in a fun way (page 7)